The title “Poetry of Comfort and Hope for the Grieving” fits Ron Tranmer’s book very well. The numerous poems offer gentle encouragement and love which speak to our hearts during the difficult time of bereavement.

“Poetry of Comfort and Hope for the Grieving” includes poems that address loss in broad terms to the more specific relationships, such as losing your spouse, infant, teenager, grandparent, etc.

While these poems acknowledge the pain of loss that all of us experience, they offer the promise of “new life” for us and our loved ones beyond our lives here on earth. They help us to focus of the promise of Heaven. Ron Tranmer also reminds us that one day we will be reunited once again with our nearest and dearest.

This book is a valuable instrument in the healing process; giving acknowledgement to our pain while at the same time giving us hope for tomorrow. Buy it for yourself or as a gift for someone close to you who is hurting.

Mary Chamberlin
www.comfort-for-bereavement.com

At the James Lawrence Company, we supply gifts to retailers around the globe. In our “Traditions” line of wall plaques we feature the poetry of Ron Tranmer. Ron’s heartfelt poems bring words of comfort and appreciation to the ones we love. He has a wonderful writing style, and we are pleased to endorse his book, “Poetry Of Comfort & Hope for The Grieving”.

Brian Johnson – General Manager
James Lawrence Co. Ltd.

In my 38 years as a funeral director I have often seen myself as working near that portal between this life and the next, this world and the next. I have seen that the purpose of my work is to be of assistance to those left on this side. Ron's simple, unpretentious poetry presents thoughts and feelings from both sides. His words come from experience and faith and give a richer meaning to the expression, "circle of life". They impart both comfort and hope. I know that many grieving people will benefit from opening their hearts to his message.

John Conroy
Hope Memorial Chapel
Biddeford, Maine

Dear Ron,

How can I thank you for your book, "Poetry Of Comfort & Hope". It is a treasure. It surely brought comfort and peace to my heart as soon as I started reading it. What a wonderful gift you have!

Luana

Hi Mr. Tranmer,

When I read your poetry, it gives me a sense of inner peace, You clearly have a gift, and I thank God for poets and authors with such talent like you.

Thank you,,,
Jane

Inspirational Poetry of Comfort & Hope for The Grieving

by Ron Tranmer

(Author of "Broken Chain")

THIS BOOK IS DEDICATED TO MY DAD,

WALTER J. TRANMER,

(For whom I wrote, "Final Footsteps", and "Slipping Away")

AND TO MY GRANDSON,

JORDAN DAVIS.

(For whom I wrote, "TEARDROPS", AND "S.I.D.S.")

I AM SO VERY GRATEFUL TO MY SAVIOR, AND REDEEMER, JESUS CHRIST FOR HIS ATONING SACRIFICE, WHICH ASSURES US OF ETERNAL LIFE, AND FOR THE KNOWLEDGE THAT WE WILL AGAIN SEE OUR DECEASED LOVED ONES WHEN WE LEAVE THIS LIFE.

About Me

I was born in Jerome Idaho in 1940, the oldest of seven children. I have been married to an angel for 53 years. We have 4 children, 13 grandchildren, and 8 great-grandchildren.

I have always enjoyed writing poetry. I wrote my first poem when I was eight years old for the prettiest girl in my class. It got a big smile so I was inspired to write more. I wrote "Broken Chain" at the passing of a family member, and "Teardrops" when we lost a grandchild. Over the years I have written, and copyrighted, over 300 poems on many different subjects, and for many occasions. Many are licensed and can be found on wall plaques, woven throws, headstones, cups, bookmarks, and music boxes. It is through the encouragement of family members, and many funeral directors, that this book has come about.

The greatest happiness I find in my writing comes from the many messages I receive telling me of the comfort one of my poems has given to someone who has lost a loved one. I hope my thoughts, put to rhyme, helps to remind us of the importance of God, family, friendship, love, and compassion in our lives.

If you are grieving, I sincerely hope you find comfort as you read through this book. I realize not all the poems in the book may not relate to your specific loss, and some may conflict with your particular religious beliefs, but it is my hope that you find at least one or two that fit perfectly, and bring you comfort & hope.

Putting words
On paper to
Express in part,
Thoughts from me
Right to
Your heart

There's something about the power of poetry to bring understanding and comfort at a time of loss. It can help break the bands of grief, and reminds us that death is not the end and that our loving Father in Heaven has a plan, which in time will bring us together again with loved ones.

Personal Note

If we truly believe that we are the children of God, and that He loves us, we must also believe that our Father In Heaven has a purpose for us. He placed us here upon the Earth to gain experience, and expects us to return to Him when our life is over. We are a part of His Heavenly family.

He has also given us families here on Earth, and I am convinced scripture supports my belief that family bonds on this Earth are not dissolved at the end of our mortal lives, but the bonds of love we develop here on Earth will live forever.

A verse in my "Family Tree" poem reads:

> *"For when our Father calls us home*
> *How great our joy will be*
> *In finding loved ones waiting there*
> *On Heaven's family tree."*

I believe this with all my heart.

Baby & Child Section

A Beautiful Day In Heaven

Death is but a passing
from darkness into light.
I awakened from my sleep
and beheld a glorious sight.

It's a beautiful day in Heaven.
Love is everywhere.
Peace and joy surround me.
Earth cannot compare.

I could never begin to describe
the wondrous things I see.
If you could glimpse at heaven,
you'd shed no tears for me.

Keep my memory in your heart.
Time will pass and then,
one beautiful day in Heaven
we'll be together again.

A Better Place

Your light no longer shines on earth,
but glows in Heaven's skies.
While Heaven is rejoicing,
tears are falling from my eyes.

I love you beyond measure.
It's so hard to let you go.
I am going to miss you
much more than you could know.

You touched the hearts of everyone
on earth you ever knew,
with acts of love and kindness
which are typical of you.

The memory of your life
will remain forever dear.
The world is a better place
because you tarried here.

All Live Again

All who live upon the earth
shall surely die someday.
But death does not end life
when these bodies pass away.

The spirit shall go on to live,
and will forevermore,
without the fragile body
which was it's home before.

As mortals, we are left behind
with sorrow, and with pain,
but grateful to our Savior,
for through Him all live again!

A Perfect World

In a perfect world,
death would never be.
Life would be forever
throughout eternity.

In a perfect world
you'd still be by our side,
lighting up our happy lives.
You never would have died.

In a perfect world
pain would not be found,
but joy, love, and happiness
forever would abound.

We believe that perfect world
awaits us when we die.
A world where eternal bliss
is found in Heaven's sky.

With faith, we wait until the day
we pass through golden gates,
and join you there in heaven
where our perfect world awaits.

A Time For Goodbye

There's a time for us to live,
and a time when we must die.
There's a time to say hello,
and a time to say goodbye.

Although it's very hard
to tell you goodbye now,
we'll wipe away our tears
and continue on somehow.

Then when our lives are over
and it's time for us to go,
they'll be telling us goodbye
as we're telling you hello.

Angel Mother

Mom, you look so pretty today
as you lie there in sleep.
All dressed up in your best dress
while I stand here and weep.

I always knew this day would come,
but still it's hard to bear.
Seeing the mom I love so much
lifelessly lying there.

It was you who gave me birth
and taught me how to love.
For your life and great example,
I thank you, and God above.

There's never been another in
this world who could compare.
Rest well, my angel mother.
I know you're in God's care.

Because I Love Her Too

I took someone you dearly love
somewhere that's far from you.
I called her home to be with me
because I love her too.

I feel your pain and sadness,
but let your faith be strong.
The one you love is in my care
and joyfully lives on.

Weep because you miss her
and because you're far apart.
These are feelings from the love
I've placed inside your heart.

In time I'll send an angel
to come to earth for you,
and bring you here to be with us,
because I love you too.

Before I Said Goodbye

God quickly called your name
and to Heaven you did fly,
before I had a chance to say
"I Love You," and "Goodbye."

I know that they are words
you've often heard before,
but how I wish I could have
spoken them to you once more.

I can only hope you know
how much you mean to me.
You've always been my hero
and forever you will be.

May an angel take this message
all the way to heaven's sky.
"I'll love you for forever.
'Till we meet again... Goodbye."

Box Of Hearts

What will you do with all the hearts
that went to heaven with you?
They knew they had to tag along
or stay and break in two.

Although our hearts went with you,
loving memories stayed behind,
where they'll remain forever,
deeply cherished in our minds.

When you are thinking of us
from your heavenly home above,
just open up your box of hearts,
and you will feel our love.

Broken Chain

We little knew the day that God
was going to call your name.
In life we loved you dearly.
In death we do the same.

It broke our hearts to lose you
but you didn't go alone.
For part of us went with you
the day God called you home.

You left us peaceful memories.
Your love is still our guide,
and though we cannot see you,
you are always at our side.

Our family chain is broken
and nothing seems the same,
but as God calls us one by one
the chain will link again.

Broken Chain

(Revised)

We little knew that day
God would call your name.
In life we loved you dearly.
In death we do the same.

It broke our hearts to lose you
but you didn't go alone.
For part of us went with you
the day God called you home.

We're left with loving memories
of the time we had together,
and will keep you in our hearts
forever and forever.

Our family chain is broken
and nothing seems the same,
but as God calls us one by one
the chain will link again.

By My Side

Oh, what would I do, dear Lord
without Thee by my side,
comforting my grieving heart
when one I love has died?

I'm so grateful for Thy love,
and for Christ, Thy Son.
Because of His great sacrifice
eternal life is won.

My heart is overflowing
with gratitude to Thee,
for in my time of sorrow
Thou hast walked with me.

Dad's Promise

As our dear dad lay dying,
we stood at his bed and wept.
It was there he made a promise
to you Mom, which he kept.

He spoke so very softly
we drew close so we could hear.
He was growing weaker
and we knew his time was near.

Dad's final words to you Mom,
were words which we heard too.
He promised, God be willing,
when you died he'd come for you.

Years passed quickly since that day,
and God called you to go.
You smiled before you closed your eyes.
Dad came for you... we know.

Do You Know?

Do you know how much I miss you?
Do you know how much I've cried?
Do you know how very much I long
to have you by my side?

Do you miss me there in Heaven?
Can you see the tears that flow?
I await the day God calls my name.
I love you so much...

Do you know?

Empty Chair

There's an empty chair at our table.
A missing leaf from our family tree.
A break in our family circle.
An empty feeling inside of me.

You've left our family here on earth,
and friends who hold you dear.
Your spirit is in paradise,
but in our hearts you're near.

God gave us families here on Earth
to cherish and to love,
and one by one He'll call us
to our Heavenly home above.

Where chairs will be filled at our table.
Every leaf will be on our tree.
Our family circle will be complete
and how great our joy will be!

When it becomes our time to die,
a tear shall come to someone's eye.
But peace comes when we understand,
death is a part of God's great plan.

For on the morrow we shall see
that dying sets our spirits free.
and when we walk through heavens door,
we'll live in joy forevermore.

So friends and family dry your eyes,
and think no more of sad goodbyes.
Rejoice, because of Christ, God's Son.
Through Him, Eternal Life is won.

Faith, Hope, Charity

At A Time Of Loss

Faith *in knowing our loved one*
is in a wonderful place,
waiting for that happy day
when we'll again embrace.

Hope *that soon we'll overcome*
The grief that we now feel.
That God will bring us comfort,
and help our hearts to heal.

Charity *is pure sweet love,*
and through our time of sorrow,
the love of family, and of friends,
will help us face tomorrow..

Family Tree

There's love within our family tree
where happiness abounds.
Our roots are deeply planted
in rich and fertile grounds.

We enjoy the rays of sunshine
and endure the winds and rain,
and when a leaf falls from our tree,
together we share the pain.

God gives us loving families
and never did intend,
that bonds of love we build on earth
upon our deaths should end.

For when our Father calls us home,
how great our joy will be,
in finding loved ones gathered there
on Heaven's family tree.

Fearless

I have no fear of life
and I have no fear of death.
I will be at peace the day
I breathe my final breath.

For I have done my very best
to live life righteously.
In life I walked with God.
In death He'll walk with me.

Written at the passing of my father/ by Ron Tranmer

With pain in my heart and tears in my eyes,
I walk to your casket to tell you goodbye.
It becomes harder with each step I take.
I'm afraid my poor heart is going to break.

I cannot describe the emotions I feel.
I love you so much, and I always will.
No one in this world has meant more to me.
Each step that I take is pure agony.

You've always been there cheering me on.
I just can't believe that now you are gone.
You were my hero. The best friend I had.
It's hard now to say goodbye to you, Dad.

Tears are now flowing over my cheeks.
My footsteps are slowing and I'm feeling weak.
As I take my last step and your face I can see,
a sweet peaceful feeling came quickly to me.

Although your body lies lifelessly here,
I know you live on. I feel you so near.
Your spirit touched mine. My heart will mend.
Goodbye for now Dad. I'll see you again.

Finding Comfort

Oh, how much I miss you,
and wish you were still here,
but I find comfort in our God
and feel His presence near.

He knows how great my sorrow.
His Son died on Earth too.
It was here He suffered all
for love of me and you.

Because of Christ's Atonement
I know you yet live on
in a place of happiness
where suffering is gone.

Death is the door to eternal life,
and one we'll all walk through.
When time opens it for me,
I'll be again with you.

Forever Love

Heaven is a place of love
if heaven is to be...
For it would not be heaven
If you're not there with me.

Forever Tomorrow

Today will have an ending,
as did yesterday.
But tomorrows are forever
and will never go away.

Tomorrow will bring sunshine,
and dry out today's rain.
Tomorrow will bring happiness,
and take away our pain.

In the future of tomorrow
we too shall pass away,
and then again be with the one
whose life we mourn today.

Tomorrow brings eternal life,
where we'll be free from sorrow.
With faith, look to a brighter day,

Somewhere...

Sometime...

Tomorrow.

For They Shall Be Comforted

*Bonds of love made here on earth
grow deep within our hearts,
and death brings pain and suffering
when one we love departs.*

*If not for love within our hearts
death would not bring grief,
and someone's passing would be as
the falling of a leaf.*

*It is good for us to mourn
when one we love has died,
for grieving shows compassion
and a loving heart inside.*

*In the Sermon on the Mount,
our Savior, Jesus, said;
"Blessed are they who mourn,
for they shall be comforted."*

(Matthew: 5,4)

Gentle Breeze

I placed a flower upon her grave
and ask dear God above,
"Why Lord did you take from me
the one I dearly love?

I need her more than heaven.
There are many angels there.
To take my angel from the earth
has left me in despair."

As I prayed and cried in anguish
there appeared a gentle breeze,
and I thought I heard a whisper
as I knelt there on my knees.

"Put all faith and trust in me,
for death is not the end.
Time will quickly pass and then
you'll be with her again."

The wind went softly on its way
whistling through the trees,
and I found the peace I sought
in a fleeting, gentle breeze.

God gave us beautiful flowers
and tall majestic trees.
The warming rays of sunshine
and the coolness of a breeze.

Bright rainbows of all colors
that please the human eye,
and endless shining stars
that twinkle in the sky .

The seashore, and the oceans
ever rolling waves of blue.
Then from above, a gift of love...
He blessed the world with you!

We thank dear God in Heaven
for the time that you were here.
We'll love you for forever
and hold your memory dear.

We know there's yet another gift
our Father has in store.
One we'll receive the bless'ed day
you're in our arms once more.

Happy Birthday In Heaven

Happy Birthday up in Heaven
from your family here below.
We love you and we miss you,
and want to let you know.

Your birthdays aren't forgotten.
Your memory yet lives on.
We still celebrate your life
even though you've gone.

If we could send a present
to your heavenly home above,
it would be a pretty basket,
filled with all our love.

Heaven's Key

Death is but a golden key
that opens Heaven's door.
Every living soul will die then
live forevermore.
Although parting brings
great sorrow
To loved ones left behind,
trust in
Him who sent us here,
and comfort we shall find.

His Love

The day God called your name
I felt I too had died.
I didn't think I could go on,
and many tears I cried.

I wondered why He would take one
as wonderful as you...
Then in my heart I heard Him say,
"Because I love her too."

In my grief, I failed to trust
in Father up above.
He calls us home to be with him
because of His great love.

How Far Is Heaven?

How far away is heaven?
Is it as far as distant stars?
Or maybe even further...
Past the moon, or even mars?

It could be a billion miles,
yet we're never far apart.
You may have left the world
but you'll never leave my heart.

I Believe

I believe the gates of Heaven
opened wide with you in view.
And golden trumpets sounded
as Saint Peter bid you through.

That angel's choirs were singing
and happiness filled the air.
And God our Father, and His son,
came to greet you there.

I envision them embracing you
and telling you, "Well done.
Come enter into glory,
our faithful precious one".

If Heaven Is

If Heaven is a special place
where we will find God's best...
A place where those who love Him
will find joy, and peace, and rest...

If Heaven is a place for those
who followed Christ, His son,
and lived their lives with kindness
and love for everyone...

If Heaven is a beautiful place
where wonderful people go
to be with God forevermore...
Then you are there, I know.

I Imagine Heaven

I imagine Heaven
as a peaceful happy place,
where joy and contentment
puts a smile on every face.

I imagine many mansions
and streets of shining gold.
Never being sick again,
and never growing old.

I imagine Heaven
as a paradise above.
A perfect place where every heart
is filled with pure sweet love.

I imagine Heaven as a place
where dreams come true.
A place where I will one day share
eternity with you.

Life After Life

Though parting brings great sadness
when we lose someone who's dear,
knowing death is not the end
brings comfort to each tear.

We pass on to a better world
where cares and sorrows flee,
and in our life after this life
how great our joy will be.

There is life after life,
so death where is thy sting?
We will live forever
because of Christ, our King.

Life's In ~ Between

All who live upon the earth
in time shall pass away,
and return to God their maker
to be judged on judgment day.

From the day that we are born
our death is unforeseen,
but birth and death dates matter not.
What counts is in-between.

One who we all dearly love
has left this place called earth.
God has watched her "in-between"
and knows how great her worth.

A life lived so unselfishly
with love for everyone,
will be taken up to Heaven
and the mansion she has won.

Living Memory

No one ever really dies,
for even though they've gone,
Somewhere in someone's heart
their memory yet lives on.

Lonely Word

"Goodbye" is such a lonely word,
It should be thrown away.
The words, "See you later"
are words I'd rather say.

Look Up

Look up
when life is getting you down
and you are sad and blue.

Look up
and know that God above
is watching over you.

Look up
When heartaches come your way
and seem to fill your cup.

His sweet love will bring you peace
if only you'll

Look Up.

Longing

My heart feels like it's broken.
Much sorrow fills my brain.
My eyes are red from crying.
My tears come down like rain.

My hands are clasped together
as I pray that I'll be strong.
My legs would like to take me
up to Heaven, where you've gone.

My arms still long to hold you
just as they used to do.
My lips long for one last kiss…

Oh, how I'm missing you.

Love Beyond Compare

I often look up to the sky
and ask my Lord and Savior why
He would suffer, bleed, and die
for someone such as me.

For my sins did Christ atone.
His sacrifice for me has shown
the greatest love I've ever known.
A love beyond compare.

Although nothing could repay
the gift he gave upon that day
I'll try to live in such a way
He'll see my gratitude.

Then when I die, my soul will flee
because of what He did for me,
and I shall live eternally
in joy and peace above.

Memories

Memories of you linger.
Your voice, your touch, your smile.
These happy loving memories,
will sustain me for a while.

Then time 's fading memories
will be fresh as summer rain,
on the day God calls me home
to be with you again.

Memories And Your Photograph

Together we are one,
and without you I am half.
I'm left with only memories,
and a favorite photograph.

You are always on my mind.
My thoughts are just of you.
You were the best part of my life.
Our love was pure and true.

Your picture's worth a thousand words,
but to me there are but three.
The simple words, "I Love You",
keep coming back to me.

I grieve the day
he passed away.
My Father

He left this Earth,
one of great worth.
My Father

I thank God, who gave him to me.
A better father could never be.
Again one day I know I'll see
My Father

Take him there
into Thy care.
My Father

Until the day
I go the way
Of Father

Then what joy will take place
when I see his smiling face,
and loving arms reach to embrace...
My Father

New Dawn

A new dawn welcomes
a beautiful day
for the one I love,
who has just passed away.

Home to our Father
to live evermore,
and to family and friends
who have passed on before.

Pain, and all suffering
forever will cease.
Instead only happiness,
comfort, and peace.

While I am mourning
my loved one lives on.
Awakened with glory
in Heaven's new dawn.

Open Doors

He used to open doors for her
with gentlemanly grace.
He used to take her out to eat
to their old favorite place.

He used to always hold her hand
and squeeze it nice and tight,
while whispering, "I love you",
at a movie on "date night".

He used to bring her flowers
in a beautiful bouquet.
"I'll love you for forever",
is what the card would say.

When It grew time to leave behind
the one he loved so true.
He whispered, "Heaven waits for me,
and there I'll wait for you."

The years passed by and when she died
there he was in wait,
opening wide for his sweet love,
Heaven's golden gate.

Papa you have left me
with something I hold dear.
The sweet & precious memory
of you, while you were here.

You'll always were a hero.
(at least one in my eyes.)
My Papa could do anything...
and no one was as wise.

I often wonder, Papa,
if you ever really knew
the love and admiration
I have always had for you.

I love you so much Papa
and even though you've died,
if you could look into my heart
you'd see your still inside.

Precious One

On angels wings my loved one flies,
with graceful speed to heaven's skies.
To God's embrace, and words, "Well done...
Welcome home, my precious one."

Pretending

I placed flowers upon your grave,
as I do each time I'm there.
Then with an overflowing heart,
I said a little prayer.

I thanked my Heavenly Father
for the time I had with you,
and told Him how I miss you,
(knowing He already knew.)

I smiled, thinking of the love
and happiness we had.
Then cried, because without you
I'm lonely, and so sad.

I close my eyes as I pretend
that you are here with me
and feel your warm embrace
as you kiss me tenderly.

With every day that passes,
I celebrate it's ending,
for time will bring me there with you
and I can stop pretending.

Quietly

How quietly you left us
in the darkness of the night.
Freed from every Earthly care,
your soul has taken flight.

Although our hearts are broken,
your death is bittersweet.
Heaven is rejoicing
from your life on Earth's retreat.

You've lived a life of kindness
and are loved by all you knew.
We give thanks to God, our Father...
because He gave us you!

Real Men Cry

I attended a large funeral
of a little child who died.
The fathers heart was broken,
and openly he cried.

This man, by all who know him,
is a rugged type of guy,
and no one thought they'd ever see
this big and tough man cry.

But I thought, "Here's a man
who shows no outward fears,
and proves that he is human
by the shedding of his tears."

They who say real men don't cry
don't seem to understand;
A man who shows emotions
is by far the greater man.

If you are one who still believes
the "Men don't cry" concept,
read John Eleven: Thirty Five,
where it's written... "Jesus wept."

Roads End

My road of life came to it's end,
but do not weep and mourn, my friend.
As you think of me be glad
for all the happy times we had.

My life was blessed, my troubles few
because of family and friends like you.
I've lived and loved, and laughed and cried.
'Till your road ends... enjoy the ride.

Sad & Glad

Though my heart is filled with sadness
I have thoughts of gladness too.
Two emotions, both from love,
are in my heart for you.

I'm sad that you have passed away,
but glad you're pain is gone.
I'm sad because I'll miss you so,
and glad that you live on.

I'm sad that I'll no longer see
that smile upon your face,
but glad to know that you are well
and in a happy place.

As I think about the conflict,
I suddenly can see...
The happiness is all for you.
The sadness is for me.

Slipping Away

I think that now I'm ready to go.
I feel the time is right.
My spirit is slowly slipping away.
I may not last the night.

I've lived my life and done my best
to honor God above.
I've raised a family as I best could.
We've shared tremendous love.

I feel your presence around my bed,
and tears upon my cheek.
I wish I could express my love,
but I am just too weak.

Thank you all for loving me.
You know I love you too.
From my new home in heaven
I'll be watching over you.

In time we'll be together again.
Don't weep too long for me,
for all will live beyond the grave
into eternity.

I see a warm and glowing light
and am drawn to follow there.
I feel a happy peaceful calm
and love from everywhere.

So hold me now once more on earth
as your tears fall on my face,
and then I'll slip away in peace
Into God's loving grace.

Smile

Goodbye family and friends.
My soul has taken flight.
I'm entering the spirit world
and what a beautiful sight.

Peace and love surround me
in a way I've never known.
I have the strongest feeling
that this is my true home.

Should you be feeling sorrow,
don't weep too long for me.
From earthly cares and suffering
I have been set free.

So goodbye family and friends,
but only for a while.
Keep my memory in your hearts,
and upon your lips... A Smile.

Somewhere

Somewhere tears are falling
Someone loved has passed away.
Somewhere a heart is breaking.

...It's my heart today.

Storms Of Sadness

Today there will be rainclouds
with intermittent tears.
We'll have periods of sadness
until scattered heartache clears.

Dark clouds will hang over us
well into the night,
continuing through tomorrow.
No sunshine is in sight.

But wait... A satellite report
from Heavens tower above,
says conditions will improve
through flurries of God's love.

His great healing power
can make storms of sadness end.
If we'll but put our faith in Him,
the sun will shine again.

Sunset, Sunrise

How lovely is a sunset
at the ending of a day.
Beauty from the falling sun
can take one's breath away.

When the sun sets on our lives
and this earthly body dies,
we'll awaken to the beauty
of a glorious sunrise.

And with our new awakening
we'll find joy we've never known
in the beauty of God's Heaven,
and our new eternal home.

Take My Hand

If in my sorrow I lose sight
of Thy great love and guiding light,
take my hand, dear Lord I pray,
and comfort me along the way.

Beyond Earth's veil I cannot see,
but with much faith I'll trust in Thee.
I know in time I'll understand.
Until then Lord, please take my hand.

My purpose here may I fulfill,
and in all things, do Thy will.
The trials of life may I withstand.
Walk with me Lord and take my hand.

Then when I breathe my final breath
and close my eyes in earthly death,
may I not leave this world alone.
Take my hand and walk me home.

Teardrops And Rainbows

When sorrow comes into our lives
and tears of sadness fall,
they never go unnoticed.
God sees them one and all.

Our tears are very precious
In the eyes of our dear Lord.
He calls them up to special clouds
where they are safely stored.

When these clouds are heavy laden
from the weight which they contain,
moisture falls upon the earth
and tears come down as rain.

Then, when the rain has ended,
look to the sky above,
and when you see a rainbow
God is sending us His love.

Tears

Tears are falling from the eyes
that long to see your face.
Arms that used to hold you tight
now miss your sweet embrace.

Lips wish they could say goodbye
and kiss you just once more.
Feet would like to run to where
you are past Heaven's door.

Hearts left behind are broken
because they miss you so.
You were loved while on this earth
more than you could know.

Time will dry our falling tears
and broken hearts will mend.
And happiness will fill our hearts
when we're with you again.

The Beginning

The Time has come to say goodbye.
Such sadness here I see.
You'd think my life has ended,
but it's just begun for me.

I know that you will miss me,
but please don't be so sad.
If you but knew what I know now,
for me you'd be quite glad.

Angels are surrounding me
awaiting your goodbyes.
My spirit then will follow them
to Heavens waiting skies.

Loved ones who have gone before
are anxious as they wait
for me to leave you for a time,
and meet at heaven's gate.

My spirit is alive and well.
Death is not an ending,
but a joyful transformation
to a beautiful beginning.

The Bridge

There is a bridge that we must cross
to reach the great divide,
where peace and happiness await
there on the other side.

As we cross, we leave behind
dear friends and family.
And some will grieve because their loss
is all that they can see.

But If they knew what joy awaits
there in the great beyond,
they wouldn't feel such sorrow
when a loved one passes on.

It was God who built the bridge
that we will cross one day,
and when we do, He'll walk with us
to Heaven all the way.

The Cost Of Freedom

He died serving our country
in a land far away.
With sadness we give honor
to a hero on this day.

He loved his family more than life
and had to do what's right.
To protect them and his country,
he joined in the fight.

Lord bless this soldiers family
who has lost a brave young son.
And watch over those still fighting,
and their families, every one.

How great the cost of freedom.
How brave those who defend.
Bless our country Lord we pray,
and bring war to an end.

The Dash Between

I knelt there at the headstone
of one I love, and cried.
Name with dates of birth and death
were perfectly inscribed.

I pondered these two dates
and how little they both mean
when compared to the tiny dash
that lies there in between.

The dash serves as an emblem
of our time here on the earth
and although small, it stands for all
our years of life and worth.

And our worth will be determined
by how we live each day.
We can fill our dash with goodness,
or waste our lives away.

To ourselves, as well as others,
let's be honest, kind and true,
and every day, live the way
we know God wants us to.

May we look for opportunities
to do a worthy deed,
and reach out with compassion
to those who are in need.

For If our hearts are full of love
throughout our journey here,
we'll be loved by all who knew us
and our memory they'll hold dear.

And when we die, those memories
will bring grateful, loving tears
to all whose lives were touched
by that small dash between our years.

The Light

In the darkness of the death
of one so dearly loved,
the light of our dear Savior
shines brightly from above.

His gift of the atonement
is the light these rays transcend,
declaring to the world,
"All who die shall live again".

The Other Side

Many hearts are broken.
Many eyes have cried.
But many now rejoice with you
there on the other side.

Although I long to have you here
and wish you hadn't died,
I know there's joy and happiness
there on the other side.

With faith I'll find the needed strength
to help me make it through,
for the other side is where, one day,
I'll be again with you.

Things I Miss

I'm left with loving memories
and often reminisce
about our times together
and the many things I miss.

Your warm, contagious smile.
Your sweet and gentle touch.
And all your hugs and kisses
that meant so very much.

How beautiful and special
all my memories of you bring.
What do I miss most of all?

EVERYTHING!

Together Again

When her husband passed away
the loneliness began.
He was her life, her everything,
her sweetheart and her man.

Family and friends drew closer
but she wasn't quite the same.
They knew how much she missed him
for she often spoke his name.

She knew that God would never let
death be their last goodbye,
for true love is forever,
and doesn't end because we die.

The years rolled on, as years will do.
She sensed her time was near.
Anticipation filled her mind.
Of death she had no fear.

On the day she left us,
she smiled and said his name.
Then followed him to Heaven.
They're together once again.

Tomorrow

Although clouds have gathered
and my teardrops fall like rain,
tomorrow will bring sunshine
and take away this pain.

I know I cannot bring you back,
but one thing I can do,
is cherish every memory
of the time I had with you.

Today I'll mourn my loss
amid much grief and sorrow,
knowing through my Savior's love
the sun will shine tomorrow.

Too Young

You were much too young
to depart this mortal life,
leaving dear sweet children
and me... your loving wife.

I'm sure God knows we need you here,
but He must need you more.
With broken hearts, and faith in Him
your family will endure.

My love for you will always be,
even though you've died.
And I'll do my best to raise our kids
so you'll look down with pride,

Oh, how much I miss you,
my sweetheart and best friend.
I wait to be with you again,
for death is not the end.

Treasured Moments

I treasure every moment
you spent in life with me.
I'd hoped to have you longer
but it's not meant to be.

You left this world so suddenly.
I think my heart went too.
I have an empty feeling
and I'm lonely without you.

My life has lost all meaning.
You were my strength, my all,
but an angel called your name
and you answered Heaven's call.

I know you're in a better place
I know you're happy there.
I know one day I'll join you,
but the wait is hard to bear.

I'll wait with faith and hope
for the angel's call again,
as I pray to God for courage
to go on alone 'til then.

Troubled Heart

On the day you took your life,
we felt ours ended too.
If we could only turn back time
there's much we would undo.

We didn't see the warning signs.
You held them deep inside.
Struggles you were going through
you did so well to hide.

We're left with guilt and sorrow
and confusion as to why
you didn't tell us of your pain
and felt you had to die.

Every soul is precious
In the eyes of God above.
He will heal your troubled heart
and bless you with His love.

We will put our faith in Him,
and pray our hearts will mend.
We love you so, and know in time
we'll be with you again.

True Treasures

What brings the greatest happiness
throughout our journey here?
Of all the things we have in life
what do we hold most dear?

The answer is, for most of us,
as plain as plain can be...
Life's only real true treasures
are our friends and families.

All life's other treasures
mean nothing when we're gone,
but love for those whom we hold dear
forever will live on.

Twinkling Star

When I look up to heaven
and the stars shine down on me,
I pretend that you're the biggest,
and the brightest star I see.

I like to think that every star
shines down on those they love,
watching over us each night
from heaven's sky above.

I'm thinking as I see you
shining there so very bright,
you twinkle just to tell me
you love me, and goodnight.

Each night when I am lonely,
I know just where you are.
I look up toward the heavens
and find you… my twinkling star.

Until We Meet Again

With heavy hearts and tear filled eyes,
family and friends bid you goodbye.
Together this day united in sorrow,
yet with faith in a brighter tomorrow.

You're loved by all who've gathered here,
and though you've gone, we feel you near.
You've touched our lives in numerous ways,
and brightened all our yesterdays.

Sharing memories of you
is something that we love to do.
We laugh, we cry, with joy and pain.
Goodbye, until we meet again.

Walk With Me

My heart is grieving on this day.
One I love has passed away.
Dear Lord, how grateful I would be
if for a time, You'll walk with me.

In spite of deaths' unwelcome blow,
I thank Thee Lord for what I know.
Victory over death is won
because of Thy atoning Son.

When I too breathe my final breath,
and close my eyes in earthly death,
may I not leave this world alone.
Walk with me Lord, and take me home.

Today's the anniversary
of the day you left our side.
Loving memories linger
ever since the day you died.

We celebrate your life today
though you're no longer here.
The precious time we had with you
we hold so very dear.

We love you and we miss you,
and even though you've gone,
the celebration of your life
lives on.. and on.. and on.

When You Think Of Me

Let it be when you think of me,
you think not of the dead.
But know that I am living
and in paradise instead.

Forget about my body
lying deeply in the ground.
It will turn to ashes,
but I am still around.

Think of one who waits for you
to share eternity.
Think of one who loves you
every time you think of me.

I ask this question of Thee Lord,
"Why did she have to die?
You know how much I love her,
so please, Lord, tell me why."

"Yes, I know you love her.
Don't you know I love her too?
Have patience and one day in time
I'll give her back to you.

It may not be tomorrow,
and I cannot tell you when,
but trust in me and she will be
back in your arms again."

"Dear Lord, I pray, forgive me
for my lack of faith in Thee,
and thank You for her many years
shared with our family.

Please help me to be worthy
of Thy blessings from above,
and trust in Thy great wisdom,
and never ending love."

Wishes

I wish that I could be with you
and kiss you lovingly.
Hold you tightly in my arms
and feel you close to me.

I wish you could have stayed, my love,
forever by my side.
My life is filled with emptiness
ever since the day you died.

God hears our wishes, and ours prayers,
and I know He loves us too.
One day in time He'll grant my wish
and bring me there with you.

Baby & Child Section

You chose us for your family,
then put on your wings and flew
back where baby angels dwell,
and took our hearts with you.

A Crown Without the Thorns

You were born into our family
and we loved you right away,
but you just came for a visit
and were not meant to stay.

God sent you here to meet us
so we could feel your love,
then took you back to be with Him
in Heaven high above.

No need to face temptation
for one who is so pure.
The trials here upon the earth
are not yours to endure.

While angels cheer at your return,
your Earthly family mourns;
But proud, our child, because you've earned
A Crown Without The Thorns.

Angel In Disguise

It only took a little while
for us to realize,
God sent us an angel.
An Angel in disguise.

You didn't wear your angel wings.
(At least they didn't show),
but we knew that you were special
for your spirit had a glow.

You blessed our lives with happiness.
Taught love we'd never known.
How we wish you could have stayed,
but you were just on loan.

You chose us for your family
then put on your wings and flew
back where baby angels dwell,
and took our hearts with you.

Angel's Kiss

An Angel kissed me on the cheek
and said, "Awaken from your sleep."
To your dear family bid goodbye
and follow me to Heaven's sky.

My spirit rose, my body stayed,
the angel said, "Don't be afraid".
She took my hand, and with a smile
said, "You'll see God in just a while."

Even though I love you so
I know it's time for me to go.
God has purpose with each call
of both the old, and very small.

Mom and Daddy, I love you,
and Heavenly Father loves you too,
He'll comfort you with His great love
until you're here with us above.

Calling Home The Young

Your life was just beginning
when it came to an end.
Why God called you home so young
is hard to comprehend.

Perhaps the trials of this life
are not yours to endure.
He knows how sweet your spirit,
and He knows your soul is pure.

How blessed we were to have you
for the short time you were here.
We pray you feel how great our love
with every falling tear.

We'll keep your memory in our heart
and there it will remain.
With faith and hope we'll carry on
'til we're with you again.

He Took My Little Hand

God softly called my name
as He took my little hand.
He knew hearts would be broken,
but one day you'll understand.

For when He takes a child home
His purpose is unknown,
but all of His great mysteries
in the next life will be shown.

I'll watch over you, dear family,
from my new home above,
and every minute we're apart
we'll feel each others love.

I'm happy here in heaven
so don't weep too long for me.
In time we'll be together again,
and share eternity.

Heaven Bound

Sadness now surrounds us.
A little child departs.
In pain we cry, and ask God why
we're left with broken hearts.

While....

Angelic voices are singing.
Golden trumpets sound.
An angel is returning.
A child is Heaven bound.

Heaven's Rocking Chair

Are there rocking chairs in Heaven
where little babies go?
Do the angels hold you closely
and rock you to and fro?

Do they talk silly baby talk
to get a smile or two ,
and sing the sleepy lullabies
I used to sing to you?

My heart is aching for you,
my angel child so dear.
You brought such joy into my life
the short time you were here.

I know you're in a happy place,
and in God's loving care,
while in my dreams, I'm rocking you
in Heaven's rocking chair.

His Child Too

Though the loss of a little child
brings pain beyond compare,
we are comforted in knowing
our God has called you there.

You will always be our child,
and though we know not when,
we know in time that He
will put you in our arms again.

Like us, our Heavenly Father
has tremendous love for you.
and though it's hard to let you go
we know you're His child too.

If Only

If only I could send, my child,
a basket filled with love,
and pretty blue forget-me-nots
to your new home above.

If only I could send a hug
past every twinkling star,
and a suitcase filled with kisses
up to Heaven where you are.

If only I could rock you
as I did not long ago,
and sing just one more lullaby
before you had to go.

"If only" seem to fill my thoughts.
My heart so misses you.
With faith I wait until the time
if only's all come true.

In Your Arms Again

I sent a little child to you
from Heaven up above.
I chose you as her parents
because of your great love.

You cared for her and loved her
with a love much like my own,
and now your heart is breaking
because I've called her home.

She has a special spirit
and is much too pure to stay,
but is now part of your family
and I'll give her back one day.

I lent her to you for a time
and you fulfilled your part.
If you will put all faith in me
I'll heal your broken heart.

She's with Me now and waiting
for the day I call your name.
And when I do, she'll be with you,
back in your arms again.

Letter To Our Angel Child

May an angel take this letter
up to heaven where you are
so you will not forget you're loved,
though your new home is far.

How our hearts are aching
from the pain of missing you.
If only we could hold you
for just an hour or two.

Close your eyes a moment
and try hard not to peek.
Can you feel our arms around you,
and kisses on your cheek?

You are our little angel,
and forever you will be
an angel who is dearly loved
by all your family.

We end with hugs and kisses,
and every "X" and "O"
is put here to remind you,
Angel Child, we love you so.

xoxoxoxoxoxoxoxoxoxoxox

Lullaby

*If somewhere there in heaven
an angel should be free,
please have her rock my baby
with a lullaby from me.*

*And when my angel baby
drifts off in peaceful sleep,
place a gentle little kiss
upon her chubby cheek.*

*Then take her baby blanket,
with it's strands of woven gold,
and cover up her little toes
just in case they're cold.*

*Whisper softly in her ear,
as she dreams in clouds above,
and let her know her family
is sending all our love.*

Miscarriage

What we call miscarriage
Is hard to understand,
but God calls special babies
back with Him in Heaven's land.

He doesn't need to test them.
These angels are too pure.
The trials of this earthly life
are not theirs to endure.

But as all of God's children,
they need a family too.
An angel dwelt with you a while
because this child chose you.

A loving son or daughter
will be in your arms one day.
One who's watching over you.
Heaven's not that far away.

Trust in God, our Father,
and never forget this...
Everything has purpose
and with Him there is no "Mis."

Nothing

There is nothing in this world
that brings such happiness
as that of a little child,
to hold, love and caress.

And nothing in this world
can bring such heartfelt sorrow
as to have our child here one day,
and gone from us tomorrow.

During this time of sadness,
we must put all faith and trust
in God, our Heavenly Father,
who gave the child to us.

He knows our hearts are breaking,
and feels how great our pain,
He's our Father, and He loves us.
We will see our child again.

S.I.D.S

Sweet dear baby how I weep.
God took you home while fast asleep.
My child, you left so suddenly.
To keep you was not meant to be.

Sudden Infant Death Syndrome
takes so many babies home,
and leaves their family's in despair
breaking poor hearts everywhere.

These perfect angels come to Earth
where loving mothers give them birth.
Then back home, into God's care
until their family joins them there

Lord, In You I put all trust.
Faith at this time is such a must.
Give me strength to bear my pain,
until I hold my child again.

Soft Whisper

An angel in a robe of white
came to me as I slept last night.
She softly whispered in my ear,
"It's time for you to come, my dear.

Though time was short since you were born,
you've earned the crown without the thorns.
God knows the sweetness of your soul.
Your little spirit is pure and whole"

I asked if I could say goodbye,
to Mom and Dad who were nearby.
The angel smiled and with a nod,
said, "Yes, I'm sure that would please God."

Did you hear my soft goodbyes,
and feel the teardrops from my eyes?
Please don't weep too long for me.
My leaving now is meant to be.

Trust in God. He'll hold your hand,
and help so you will understand.
Then in His time, He'll call you too
and I'll be waiting here for you.

My dear sweet angel baby
there's so much I want to say.
You became part of our family
but were much too pure to stay.

You have a special spirit.
One too perfect for this earth.
God chose me for your mother
then took you home before your birth.

Although my heart is breaking
I put all trust in God above.
He knows that stillborn babies
still have their mother's love.

I know you're in His tender care,
and one day we will meet.
I await the happy day
our family is complete.

Teen Angel

You had everything to live for.
Love, and hope, and dreams.
Yet God's angels came for you
while only in your teens.

We are thankful that we had you
If but only for a while.
You blessed us with amazing love,
and warmed us with your smile.

We'll keep alive our memories
of happy times with you.
The places where we've been,
and the things we used to do.

We know there is a Heaven,
and that you are in Gods care.
We pray that He will comfort us
until we join you there.

Teardrops

Teardrops are falling. We 're saddened this day.
Our dear little baby has just passed away.
For such a short time we were blessed with the love
of a sweet little angel from heaven above.

Our family is grieving. We weep, and we pray.
Our hearts know the reason why you couldn't stay.
A spirit who's so special, and so perfect, and pure,
should not have the trials of this life to endure.

You wanted a family and that's why you came.
To be loved on earth, and given a name.
Then back to our Heavenly Father you went,
fulfilling the mission for which you were sent.

Although our grief is so hard to bear,
we know you are happy in heaven somewhere.
You have overcome death. You're spirit lives on.
You're a part of us still even though you have gone.

Know that we love you our dear little one.
We'll join you when God says our time here is done.
Save us a place, close by your side,
and our joy will erase all the tears that we've cried.

Teddy Bear

It's my very favorite place.
I feel closer to you there.
We rock the hours away.
Me, and your Teddy Bear.

The rocking chair is squeaking,
as rocking chairs will do.
I pretend the one I'm holding
isn't Teddy Bear, but you.

I miss your little chubby cheeks.
They were so fun to kiss.
Cuddling you, and hearing you goo
are among the things I miss.

Precious memories of you linger.
My child, I miss you so.
I hope one day my heart will heal.
It's hard to let you go.

When in time God calls me home
to be with you up there,
with joy I'll hold you in my arms
instead of Teddy Bear.

Thou Art God

Although it's hard to understand
why little children die,
we trust in Thy great love, dear Lord,
and shall not question why.

But with faith we shall go on
accepting of Thy will,
and pray Thy love and comfort
will help our hearts to heal.

Thou art God, the greatest of all,
from whom all blessings flow.
We are all Thy children
and are loved by Thee, we know.

Our precious child is in Thy care,
and though we know not when,
We believe in time, our child will be
back in our arms again.

To Bury A Child

We always took for granted,
as your parents, we'd go first.
But somehow in our family,
life's order got reversed.

Only those who've lost a child
can know how great the pain.
The extent of grief and suffering,
we never could explain.

The wisdom of our Father,
who dwells in heaven's sky,
Is well beyond that of our own
so we won't question why.

Instead, we'll put our faith and trust
in Him, and His great love,
until we're with you once again
in our new home above.

Unborn Angel

Our little baby angel,
who died before your birth;
You didn't get a chance to meet
your family here on Earth.

Now's a time of sadness.
A time for us to weep.
But we believe a time will come
when you'll be ours to keep.

Heaven has a special place
where unborn spirits go,
and even though we've never met
you're loved more than you know.

You Chose Us

You chose us for your family,
then put on your wings and flew
back where baby angels dwell,
and took our hearts with you.

God and all His Angels
now have you in their care,
and will be watching over you
until we join you there.